Loungefly Obsession

The Artistry and Allure of Collectible Bags

Asaf Iqbal

Prestige Quill Publishing

PRESTIGE
PUBLISHING
QUILL

In every bag, a story. In every stitch, a memory.
A. IQBAL

Foreword

In the realm of fashion and fandom, few names evoke as much recognition and ardor as Loungefly. This brand's uniquely crafted bags have cultivated not just followers, but enthusiasts and collectors.

My journey into the world of Loungefly began quite serendipitously. It was on a casual day that my wife's eyes caught the allure of her first Loungefly bag. This seemingly innocuous moment spiralled into an enduring passion.

Two dozen bags later, she has matched her prized possessions with corresponding purses. Her collection boasts an impressive array of Disney-inspired Loungefly bags, curated meticulously for every season—from the festive hues of Christmas to the spooky themes of Halloween. Among her prized possessions are pieces that echo cinematic magic, such as the enchanting Mickey Mouse Fantasia bag, the intriguing Villains series, and, her personal favourite, the captivating Hocus Pocus series.

In my endeavour to delve deeper into this world, I turned to digital communities where aficionados converge. The Loungefly subreddit, a thriving forum on Reddit,

welcomed me with open arms, allowing me to glean insights from its members. Their anecdotes, questions, and even photographs of treasured collections have enriched this book, providing an intimate glimpse into the Loungefly universe.

My outreach extended to several Loungefly-focused Facebook

groups. Although all the many forums remained silent, I hope to work with them on my follow up Loungefly book in the future.

In the foreseeable future, I hope to present a more detailed rendition of this book, incorporating interviews and insights directly from the vanguard of Loungefly's creative force—Funko-Loungefly.

To every reader who embarks on this journey with me, I extend my heartfelt gratitude. Loungefly's designs, to me, transcend mere fashion—they are an artistic expression, waiting to be celebrated.

I envision a time when these masterpieces will grace the halls of a museum, offering aficionados a tangible walk through history and artistry. Whether you want to rock a bag adorned with your favourite superhero or make a statement with a bold and vibrant design, you really cant go wrong with a Loungefly bag.

Thank you for allowing me to share this passion with you.

Asaf

Introduction to Loungefly

Loungefly a brand that has transformed the world of accessories since its inception in 1998. From a humble warehouse where Trevor Schultz, a visionary entrepreneur, laid the foundation for what would become an extraordinary empire.

Loungefly's rise to prominence can be attributed to its exceptional quality and exquisite designs, which have enthralled fans worldwide. Nestled in the vibrant heart of Southern California, this remarkable brand has left an indelible mark on the fashion industry by seamlessly blending style, creativity, and the allure of pop culture.

As Loungefly's innovative designs and meticulous attention to detail garnered recognition, they quickly became a brand to watch. Each milestone they achieved propelled them further towards global success, from their groundbreaking collaborations with major pop culture franchises to their expansion into international markets.

Loungefly's star was steadily ascending, captivating the hearts of fashion enthusiasts and bag collectors everywhere.

What truly sets Loungefly apart is not just their ability to create eye-catching designs but also their unwavering commitment to quality, craftsmanship, and innovation. To Loungefly, every bag is a masterpiece, meticulously crafted with the utmost care and precision. Their dedication to excellence ensures that their bags not only exude durability and longevity but also earn the loyalty and trust of their customers.

At the heart of Loungefly's success lies their meticulous design process. From the initial concept development to the final product, every step is carefully executed, ensuring that each bag emerges as a true work of art.

Drawing inspiration from diverse sources, incorporating

customer feedback, and staying attuned to trends, Loungefly's designers create bags that are not only visually stunning but also practical and functional.

Loungefly's commitment to sustainability and ethical sourcing is yet another testament to their outstanding values. Recognising the importance of protecting the environment, they integrate eco-friendly materials and implement ethical manufacturing processes. Through their beautiful bags, Loungefly strives to make a positive impact on the world, empowering individuals to carry their fashion choices with a conscience.

As Loungefly continues to push the boundaries of bag design, their dedication to customers remains unwavering. Countless stories and testimonials have poured in from Loungefly enthusiasts, emphasising the profound impact these bags have had on their lives.

More than just a brand, Loungefly has become a lifestyle, offering a means of self-expression and embracing individuality.

From its humble beginnings to its current status as a global sensation, Loungefly has redefined the landscape of bag design, captivating fashion enthusiasts and bag collectors worldwide. With their eye-catching designs, unwavering commitment to quality, and deep-rooted connections to pop culture, Loungefly stands as an unstoppable force in the fashion industry.

Funko

Funko was established in 1998 by avid toy collector Mike Becker, who began his venture at his residence in Snohomish, Washington. Becker's initial motivation came from his inability to find an affordable coin bank featuring the beloved Big Boy Restaurants mascot. Consequently, he secured the licensing rights from a Big Boy franchise in Michigan, allowing him to create his own coin banks. Unfortunately, the coin banks did not sell well, and the franchise eventually filed for bankruptcy protection. Despite these setbacks, Funko persevered by obtaining licenses to produce bobbleheads for Austin Powers, which proved to be a success, selling 80,000 units.

Following this breakthrough, Funko introduced iconic characters like the Grinch, Tony the Tiger, and the Cheerios mascot, the honeybee, as part of their product lineup. In 2005, Mike Becker sold Funko to Brian Mariotti, the company's current Chief Creative Officer. Mariotti relocated the company's headquarters from Lynnwood, Washington to a new location in Lynnwood, Washington, and significantly expanded Funko's range of licensed products. In 2011, Funko launched its popular Pop! Vinyl line of figurines, contributing to the company's impressive sales record, which exceeded $20 million by 2012.

In 2013, Fundamental Capital, a private equity firm, acquired Funko to raise funds. Subsequently, in late 2015, ACON Investments, LLC announced its acquisition of Funko from Fundamental Capital, LLC, ensuring the retention of existing staff and company leadership. As Funko continued to experience growth, it outgrew its original headquarters in Everett by 2016, prompting plans for a relocation to a downtown building that offered more space, including a retail store. In early 2017, Funko expanded its reach by acquiring British toymaker Underground Toys, which also served as its European distributor.

On August 19, 2017, Funko celebrated the grand opening of its new headquarters and flagship store, encompassing an impressive 17,000 square feet, in downtown Everett. Later that year, on November 2, 2017, Funko made its debut on the NASDAQ stock exchange. Unfortunately, the company's initial public offering experienced significant setbacks, with shares plummeting by 40 percent and raising only $125 million, marking it as one of the worst IPO performances of the 21st century.

In May 2019, Funko expanded its portfolio by acquiring Loungefly.
Continuing its growth, Funko inaugurated its second retail location in November 2019, situated in Hollywood, Los Angeles. This spacious store spans an impressive 40,000 square feet (3,700 m2) and features captivating life-size statues and meticulously crafted movie "sets."

In June 2022, Funko further bolstered its presence in the pop culture realm by acquiring Mondo, a distinguished company known for its high-end offerings.

In March 2023, Funko faced the challenge of limited warehouse capacity. Consequently, the company made the decision to dispose of excess old inventory to alleviate the strain on its storage capabilities. This step ensured more efficient operations and optimised warehouse management.

Funko's product design process takes place primarily at its headquarters in Everett, Washington, with involvement from various locations across the United States. When developing new figures, the company collaborates with licensors, in-studio artists, and fans who provide valuable input through social media platforms. This inclusive approach ensures that the final designs resonate with the target audience.

To bring these designs to life, Funko artists employ advanced software such as ZBrush to create intricate digital models. These digital models undergo thorough revisions and refinements before progressing to the next stage. The refined designs are then transformed into prototype sculptures, which are carefully crafted and prepared for evaluation by both manufacturers and licensors. This crucial step ensures that the prototypes meet the necessary quality standards and adhere to the specific requirements and guidelines set by the licensors.

Once the prototypes receive approval, the manufacturing process commences. Funko collaborates with factories located in China and Vietnam to produce the final figures. These factories employ specialised techniques and utilise high-quality materials to manufacture the collectibles with meticulous attention to detail, ensuring that each figure meets Funko's renowned standards of craftsmanship.

By following this comprehensive design and production process, Funko brings its imaginative and diverse range of collectibles to life, delighting fans and collectors worldwide with their extensive lineup of licensed pop culture products.

Brand Philosophy and Values

Loungefly doesn't play games when it comes to their brand philosophy and values. They wholeheartedly embrace their commitment to quality, craftsmanship, and innovation, setting themselves apart in the fashion industry and leaving an enduring impact on bag enthusiasts everywhere. Let's delve into what makes them exceptional, starting with their unwavering dedication to quality.

Loungefly is all about delivering exceptional products that surpass customer expectations. The moment you lay eyes on one of their bags, you can instantly sense that no compromises were made during the manufacturing process. Each material is carefully selected for its durability, ensuring that your Loungefly bag will stand the test of time, becoming your trusted companion for years to come. And their attention to detail? It's simply unrivalled.

Every stitch, zipper, and buckle is meticulously crafted, resulting in a bag that not only looks stunning but also functions seamlessly. Craftsmanship is another pillar of Loungefly's brand philosophy. They believe that bags are not mere accessories but true works of art. And they prove it time and again. Each Loungefly bag is a masterpiece, showcasing the extraordinary talent and skill of their team of artisans. From intricate embroidery to perfectly placed embellishments, you can feel the love and passion poured into every single bag. Carrying a Loungefly bag is like carrying a wearable piece of art—a delight for the senses.

But it doesn't stop there. Loungefly thrives on innovation. They continuously push the boundaries of bag design, seeking fresh and exciting ways to make their creations stand out from the crowd. Whether it's experimenting with unconventional materials, incorporating cutting-edge technology, or drawing inspiration from unexpected sources, Loungefly remains one step ahead in the realm of innovation. They understand that fashion is ever-evolving, and they strive to be at the forefront of those changes, delivering bags that are not only trendy but also timeless.

Now, you might be curious about how these principles translate into their designs and their relationships with customers and partners. Allow me to shed some light on that. Loungefly's commitment to quality, craftsmanship, and innovation permeates every facet of their brand. Their designs embody their dedication to excellence, seamlessly blending distinctive aesthetics with practical functionality. Whether you adore classic styles or revel in bold and quirky designs, Loungefly has an exquisite offering for everyone.

However, it's not solely about the bags themselves. Loungefly recognises that their customers are more than mere buyers; they are part of a vibrant community. They deeply value their customers' feedback and take it into consideration when creating new designs or refining existing ones. They actively listen to their customers' desires and tirelessly strive to exceed their expectations. This commitment to customer satisfaction has fostered an unwavering following of bag enthusiasts who not only adore their products but also feel a profound connection to the brand on a profound level.

Loungefly has collaborated with some of the biggest names in pop culture, crafting bags that celebrate beloved franchises like Disney, Marvel, and Star Wars. These partnerships not only showcase Loungefly's ability to tap into the pulse of pop culture but also exemplify their dedication to creating bags that resonate with their customers' interests and passions. It's a mutually beneficial relationship that has yielded truly iconic designs—designs that have etched themselves into the fabric of contemporary culture.

ASAF IQBAL

Funko's Diversification: From Pop! Figurines to Fashion with Loungefly

Derrick Bacca and Liz DeSilva hold distinguished positions as Senior Vice Presidents of Creative Innovation and Vision at Loungefly, a leading collectible fashion and accessory brand under the umbrella of pop culture titan, Funko.

In the wake of the global pandemic, Funko strategically pivoted its focus towards direct-to-consumer sales. The outcome was impressive: sales skyrocketed by 190%. Now, these sales constitute 11% of Funko's total. This surge significantly benefitted the brand's mainstay, collectible pop figures, whose sales soared by 137% in the second quarter, reaching $185.4 million. Loungefly also reaped the benefits of this strategic shift.

Having guided Funko since his acquisition of the company from founder Mike Becker in 2005, Brian Mariotti's leadership saw a significant change come. Mariotti transitioned from his role as CEO to Chief Creative Officer, passing the CEO baton to Andrew Perlmutter, the current president of Funko. Mariotti will remain an integral part of the company, continuing his service on the board.

During his tenure as CEO, Mariotti showed a keen eye for acquisitions. This enabled Funko to tap into new retail avenues, launching a Funko Games division for board games and adding Loungefly to its portfolio for fashion accessories and, more recently, apparel. It's noteworthy that acquiring Loungefly wasn't immediate; Mariotti pursued the brand for three years, recognising its potential as he remarked, "I just saw this amazing small company putting out the coolest backpacks and the coolest purses." Founded in 1998, Funko successfully acquired Loungefly in 2017. Two years following this, Bacca and DeSilva, bringing with them extensive experience in licensing and merchandising, joined the team. Their roles are defined as Loungefly's Vice

President of Sales, Merchandising, and Business Development, and Creative Vice President, respectively.

Loungefly's distinct offerings range from premium backpacks to wallets, with an added line of apparel and enamel pins. Their mini backpacks, often inspired by popular entertainment franchises or designed to resemble iconic characters, stand out as unique products in the market. With their deep industry expertise, Bacca and DeSilva recognised an untapped potential in Loungefly.

Their proactive approach reshaped the brand's strategy. Instead of being directed solely by major retailers, the duo took the initiative to create a core line of Loungefly products and then collaborated with retailers for exclusive designs. This strategy expansion also included partnering with smaller retailers and strengthening Loungefly's online presence. Their community-centric approach, coupled with a strong social media strategy, further solidified Loungefly's brand presence.

Emphasising quality, Bacca and DeSilva introduced features like size-inclusive straps and detailed designs with embossed metal rivets, enabling Loungefly to justify a premium price point. Under DeSilva's guidance, a talented team of artists and designers continue to create accessories that are not only fashionable but also tell a unique story.

Adding another feather to its cap, Funko has ventured into the cosmetics business with the acquisition of HipDot. Their inaugural collaboration under this new acquisition celebrates Netflix's "Wednesday," featuring a collection inspired by the series' protagonist, Wednesday Addams. Alongside Funko's iconic Pop! figurines and high-end Mondo brand collectibles, Loungefly will introduce accessories characterised by a grayscale color palette in homage to Wednesday Addams' distinct style.

These include a stripe-patterned mini backpack, crossbody, wallet, and cardholder, all crafted with twill and vegan leather trims. A mystery box of pins and makeup items will also mark

Loungefly's debut in the cosmetics sector.

Funko, with its diversified portfolio, continues to solidify its footprint in the world of pop culture collectibles and fashion. With Loungefly playing a pivotal role, the future looks promising for these interconnected brands.

Collaborations and Partnerships

In the dynamic realm of fashion, forming collaborations and partnerships is no longer just a trend but a quintessential strategy for brands to retain their edge and engage discerning consumers. At the heart of this transformative approach lies Loungefly, known for its captivating bags that bear the unmistakable mark of ingenious collaborations. With every partnership, Loungefly ingeniously taps into contemporary vibes, producing statement pieces that defy convention.

A pinnacle in Loungefly's collaborative journey is its enthralling alliance with the world of Disney. The timeless allure of Disney resonates with generations, and Loungefly astutely channels this enchantment into their bags. From classics such as Mickey and Minnie Mouse to cinematic masterpieces like 'Beauty and the Beast' and 'The Little Mermaid', Loungefly crafts a canvas for Disney aficionados to carry cherished narratives.

These designs, imbued with meticulous details, from intricate embroidery to concealed Mickey motifs, have become the epitome of artistry, turning heads globally.

Loungefly's synergy with eminent artists and designers has been pivotal to its ascendancy. Teaming up with visionary creatives, like the imaginative Jerrod Maruyama, Loungefly's bags become a fusion of innovation and art. The rendition of an artist's imagination onto these bags underscores Loungefly's commitment to precision and artisanship.

Venturing further, Loungefly's affiliations with iconic pop culture franchises have fortified their brand appeal. A prime instance is their Star Wars collection. Capturing the essence of this epic saga, from Darth Vader to the beloved R2-D2, these bags offer both a statement and a tribute for die-hard fans, embodying both style and substance.

The artistry behind these collaborations stems from a rigorous process. It starts with discerning research and pinpointing collaborators whose ethos mirrors Loungefly's commitment to creativity and unparalleled craftsmanship.

The ensuing design journey is a harmonious blend of both entities, giving life to bags that encapsulate the very essence of the partnership. From ideation to the final stitch, every Loungefly bag is a testament to collaborative genius.

Among the illustrious collaborators Loungefly has joined forces with include:

- Sanrio
- Disney
- Jujutsu Kaisen
- Paul Frank
- Lucasfilm
- Pokemon
- McDonalds
- Marvel
- The Beatles
- Harry Potter
- Lisa Frank

These partnerships have not only broadened Loungefly's horizons but also underscored its mark in the fashion ecosystem. Their bags aren't merely accessories; they're wearable narratives resonating with varied enthusiasts, from fashion mavens to pop culture aficionados.

Loungefly has redefined the essence of bags, turning them into emblematic artworks that empower wearers to flaunt their unique identity, while also connecting with beloved brands and narratives.

So, when you next encounter a Loungefly creation, know it's more than a bag—it's a symbol of a prolific collaboration, celebrating the spirit of creativity and passion.

Design Process

In the creative crucible of Loungefly's design studio, a transformative process unfolds where raw imagination metamorphoses into exquisite bags that resonate with aficionados worldwide.

Ever pondered the alchemy behind transforming a nascent idea into a tangible masterpiece? Let's embark on an insightful expedition to uncover the captivating evolution of Loungefly's design marvels.

The genesis of every Loungefly creation is rooted in concept development—a vibrant tapestry of ideas crafted by their brilliant designers. Drawing from the multifaceted realms of fashion, they scout the zeitgeist of popular culture: films, series, comics, and video games serve as fountains of inspiration, acting as conduits to distill the charisma of cherished characters and sagas. Merging this external muse with their intrinsic flair, the designers craft a plethora of vibrant concepts, each an embodiment of unfettered creativity.

Yet, at Loungefly, the genesis is but a fraction of the journey. Recognising the immense value of their discerning clientele's insights, the brand cultivates a symbiotic dialogue.

They attentively gather and assimilate feedback, honing their designs to reflect the aspirations and desires of those who will don their creations. This co-creative ethos ensures every Loungefly bag is not just a product but a shared vision.

The ensuing phase is where the abstract morphs into the tangible. Exemplifying unparalleled craftsmanship, the designers immerse themselves in the minutiae. Each bag's silhouette, palette, materials, and design elements are evaluated and reimagined with relentless fervour. Patterns, textures, and accents are interwoven with finesse, crafting a balance that marries form with function.

Throughout this journey, Loungefly's unwavering adherence to their brand's ethos shines through. Their undying devotion to quality, artistry, and innovation resonates in each creation.

For them, a bag transcends being a mere accessory—it stands as a testament to art. Their meticulous artisanship and pursuit of perfection culminate in designs that are both visually arresting and functionally impeccable.

Aware of the ephemeral nature of fashion trends, Loungefly constantly recalibrates its compass. Staying attuned to the pulsating rhythm of the fashion realm, they adeptly infuse emergent styles, palettes, and patterns, ensuring their bags always echo contemporary elegance.

From the conception of an idea to its final manifestation, Loungefly's design odyssey interlaces customer insights, trend analyses, and a broad spectrum of inspirations. The outcome? Bags that are more than just fashion statements—they become intrinsic extensions of the individuals they adorn.

So, the next time you witness a Loungefly bag in its splendid glory, cherish its concealed tale—a saga of fervent designers, blending their passion and expertise to birth the extraordinary.

Each design stands as a testament to a team that melds art and utility, sculpting timeless marvels in the ever-evolving world of fashion.

Materials and Production

In the intricate world of fashion, Loungefly, a highly distinguished bag manufacturer, stands tall as a shining example of how the careful selection of materials and conscientious production techniques can lead to the creation of sustainable and exemplary products. Join us on an enlightening journey behind the scenes to discover the distinct components of Loungefly's unique materials and production process that sets them a class apart from their competitors.

With an unyielding commitment to top-grade materials, Loungefly makes no compromises when it comes to sourcing the highest quality fabrics, leathers, and hardware.

Their dedication to sustainability shines through in their precise and thoughtful choice of materials. For example, the brand consciously opts for vegan leather, a material that encapsulates luxury in its look and feel, while simultaneously representing their deep-rooted values of ethical sourcing and animal rights. In choosing to utilise vegan leather, Loungefly creates bags that are not just environmentally friendly, but also a testament to their commitment to cruelty-free fashion.

Loungefly's sustainability ethos goes beyond material choices. The brand proactively employs green production methods to minimise waste and curb their carbon emissions. Through inventive recycling initiatives and energy usage optimisation, Loungefly crafts bags that are more than mere fashion accessories, they are tangible representations of environmental stewardship.

Their manufacturing process, distinguished by a rigorous attention to detail and superior craftsmanship, sets Loungefly apart. Each bag is subjected to an exhaustive quality control procedure, confirming its adherence to Loungefly's high standards of excellence. Every facet, from the precision of the stitching to the robustness of the hardware, undergoes meticulous scrutiny, yielding a product that is aesthetically pleasing and built to last. This unwavering commitment to quality is one of the key factors that differentiates Loungefly from their competition, reinforcing their esteemed reputation for superior craftsmanship.

In addition, Loungefly places a high premium on partnering with suppliers who share their ethical values. By fostering relationships with such suppliers, Loungefly guarantees the integrity of their products. These suppliers are committed to observing fair labor practices and advocating safe work environments, ensuring that the manufacturing process promotes human welfare.

This commitment to societal advancement and employee empowerment is woven into every Loungefly product, leaving a positive impact that extends well beyond their captivating designs.

But what is the significance of all this? It lies at the very core of Loungefly's company ethos. Their dedication to sustainability, ethical sourcing, and top-tier production methods is not just about creating superior products. Loungefly recognises the deep-seated effect the fashion industry has on our environment and those involved in production. Their conscious decisions and accountability set a benchmark in the industry, advocating for a more responsible and empathetic approach to fashion.

So, the next time you spot someone donning a Loungefly bag, pause to admire not just the stunning design, but also the considerate and thoughtful process behind its creation.

Loungefly's materials and production methods are a testament to their steadfast commitment to sustainability, ethical practices, and remarkable craftsmanship. Given these reasons, it's hardly surprising that Loungefly is a cherished brand among fashion connoisseurs, bag enthusiasts, and pop culture fans the world over.

19

For those new to Loungefly collecting, here are some key terms to familiarise yourself with:

- **AOP (All Over Print)**: Refers to designs printed haphazardly all over a bag.
- **Placement**: Refers to the positioning of the design, especially on the front pocket.
- **Chibi**: A character design resembling a Funko pop, characterised by exaggerated heads and tiny bodies.
- **Cosplay Bags**: Designs mimicking a character's face or attire.
- **Grail**: A highly desired bag, either personally or within the community.
- **HTF**: An abbreviation for 'Hard To Find'.
- **MMMA/MTMA**: Initialisms relating to themed merchandise releases from Disney parks.

∞ ∞ ∞

Unique Bag Designs

When it comes to bag designs that are truly unique, Loungefly reigns supreme. There bags transcend mere functionality and become captivating works of art that instantly captivate the attention of fashion enthusiasts. Loungefly understands that a bag is more than just an accessory; it is a canvas for creative expression and an embodiment of innovative design concepts.

One of the standout features that sets Loungefly bags apart is their exceptional use of patterns. From bold and vibrant prints to subtle and intricate designs, Loungefly's bags are a testament to their mastery of artistic expression.

Whether it's a whimsical floral pattern, a mesmerising geometric motif, or a captivating print inspired by pop culture, Loungefly knows how to make a statement with their patterns. These designs not only catch the eye but also inject personality and individuality into any outfit.

Colours play a vital role in the visual impact of Loungefly bags. The brand is known for their fearless and vibrant color choices, injecting an element of fun and playfulness into their designs. From eye-catching neons that demand attention to sophisticated pastels that exude elegance, Loungefly knows how to create bags that leave a lasting impression. Their thoughtfully curated color combinations ensure that each bag stands out from the crowd and becomes an expression of personal style.

Loungefly's commitment to using high-quality materials further distinguishes their designs. Their bags are crafted from materials that not only look stunning but also stand the test of time. From the luxurious feel of vegan leather to the sturdiness of canvas, Loungefly ensures that their bags are not only visually appealing but also durable and long-lasting. This meticulous attention to detail sets them apart from the rest and resonates with fashion enthusiasts who appreciate the artistry of craftsmanship.

The overall visual impact of Loungefly bags is nothing short of extraordinary. Their designs possess a unique and distinctive style that is instantly recognisable. Loungefly has mastered the art of creating bags that make a lasting impression and become a true reflection of personal taste. Whether it's a chic backpack, a trendy crossbody, or an elegant tote, Loungefly bags exude a sense of flair and individuality that sets them apart from the masses.

These are just a few examples of the unique and captivating bags that Loungefly has created through their collaborations and design expertise. Each bag embodies the brand's commitment to innovation, attention to detail, and the ability to bring beloved characters and themes to life in a fresh and exciting way:

Loungefly x Disney Villains Backpack: This backpack features an eye-catching design showcasing iconic Disney villains like Maleficent, Ursula, and the Evil Queen. The combination of bold colours, intricate details, and villainous motifs make this bag a true standout.

Loungefly x Star Wars Millennium Falcon Crossbody Bag: Inspired by the legendary starship from the Star Wars franchise, this crossbody bag captures the essence of the Millennium Falcon in stunning detail. The bag features a metallic design with intricate stitching that replicates the ship's iconic exterior.

Loungefly x Marvel Groot Mini Backpack: This mini backpack pays homage to the lovable tree-like character Groot from the Guardians of the Galaxy. The bag features a 3D Groot design with expressive eyes, detailed bark texture, and even a miniature pot on the front pocket.

Loungefly x Harry Potter Hogwarts Castle Tote Bag: Harry Potter fans will appreciate this tote bag that showcases the majestic Hogwarts Castle. The bag features a beautiful illustration of the castle, complete with iconic elements like the Quidditch pitch, the Whomping Willow, and the Great Hall.

Loungefly x Pokémon Poké Ball Crossbody Bag: Pokémon enthusiasts will adore this crossbody bag inspired by the iconic Poké Ball. The bag replicates the design of the Poké Ball, complete with the red, white, and black color scheme and the button in the centre.

Loungefly x Disney Pixar Up Balloon House Mini Backpack: This mini backpack pays homage to the beloved film Up, featuring the iconic floating balloon house. The bag showcases vibrant colours, intricate embroidery, and even includes a miniature Carl and Russell figurine on the front pocket.

Loungefly x Sanrio Hello Kitty Milk Carton Crossbody Bag: This adorable crossbody bag resembles a milk carton, with Hello Kitty's face playfully peering out. The bag features a pastel pink color, cute bow details, and a detachable strap for versatile styling.

It's no wonder that fashion enthusiasts are drawn to Loungefly bags. Their designs speak to those who appreciate the artistry and craftsmanship behind designer accessories. Loungefly understands that fashion goes beyond following trends; it is a means of self-expression and embracing one's individuality. Their bags serve as a platform for fashion enthusiasts to showcase their unique style and stand out from the crowd.

Loungefly's brand philosophy revolves around innovative design concepts. They constantly push boundaries and think outside the box to create bags that not only mesmerise with their visual appeal but also excel in functionality and practicality. Loungefly stays ahead of the curve by continuously innovating and embracing new design concepts, recognising that fashion is a dynamic and ever-evolving landscape.

So, whether you're a fashion enthusiast looking to express your creativity through accessories or a bag collector in search of limited-edition pieces that make a statement, Loungefly has something extraordinary to offer.

Their bags are a testament to the power of art and design, and they have made a significant impact in the fashion industry. With their unparalleled use of patterns, bold color choices, premium materials, and overall visual impact, Loungefly has successfully carved out a niche as a brand that celebrates creativity and innovation. So, why settle for ordinary when you can carry a bag that is a true masterpiece? Loungefly is here to redefine what it means to be fashionable, one unique bag at a time.

And remember, in a world full of monotony, life is too short for boring bags!

Let Loungefly be your guide to unlocking your style potential and allowing your creativity to soar.

Staying Ahead of the Trends

In the ever-changing landscape of fashion, staying ahead of the trends is a paramount factor for brands to remain relevant and innovative. Loungefly, the renowned bag company, has mastered the art of anticipating and embracing emerging trends, propelling them to the forefront of the industry. With their distinctive designs and ability to capture the spirit of pop culture, Loungefly has become a global sensation among fashion enthusiasts, bag collectors, and pop culture fans alike. So, what sets them apart and keeps them ahead of the curve?

One of the key elements that fuels Loungefly's success is their acute awareness of fashion trends. They possess a keen understanding of what's hot and what's not, ensuring that their bag designs align with the latest fashion movements. From bold patterns and vibrant colours to minimalist and sleek aesthetics, Loungefly's bags continuously evolve to meet the dynamic demands of fashion-forward consumers.

However, Loungefly's design inspiration goes beyond just fashion trends. They draw from the vast realm of pop culture, recognising the profound impact of nostalgia and the deep connection fans have with their favorite movies, TV shows, comics, and video games. Through collaborations with major franchises like Disney, Marvel, and Star Wars, Loungefly taps into the immense popularity of these properties, creating bags that are highly sought after by pop culture enthusiasts. These collaborations not only keep Loungefly's designs fresh and exciting, but also enable them to connect with a wider audience that shares a passion for fandom and collecting.

Consumer preferences also play a pivotal role in shaping Loungefly's designs. They understand that their customers have diverse tastes and styles, and they strive to cater to a broad range of preferences. By actively incorporating customer feedback and attentively listening to their audience, Loungefly ensures that their bags not only reflect current trends but also fulfil the needs and desires of their loyal customer base. Whether it's a particular coloruway, a specific pattern, or a unique feature, Loungefly takes customer preferences into account, ensuring that their designs resonate deeply with their target audience.

Furthermore, Loungefly's commitment to innovation is a driving force behind their ability to stay ahead of the trends. They consistently push the boundaries of bag design by exploring new materials, techniques, and concepts to create truly exceptional and attention-grabbing pieces. Whether it involves experimenting with unconventional fabrics, incorporating cutting-edge technology, or embracing sustainable and ethical practices, Loungefly remains at the forefront of innovation in the industry.

Mastering the art of staying up to date with trends in a rapidly evolving market is no small feat. It requires agility, adaptability, and an in-depth understanding of the industry. Loungefly achieves this by adopting a holistic approach to trend forecasting. They not only monitor fashion runways and attend trade shows but also closely observe social media, street style, and even emerging subcultures. By attentively tracking a diverse range of influences, Loungefly can anticipate shifts in the market and create designs that are at the vanguard of trends.

So, the next time you come across a Loungefly bag that perfectly aligns with your style or reflects your fandom, remember that behind that piece lies a world of trend forecasting, pop culture influence, and customer preferences. Loungefly's ability to stay ahead of the curve and remain innovative in a rapidly changing market is a testament to their unwavering dedication, boundless creativity, and commitment to delivering exceptional bags that deeply resonate with their audience.

So, why compromise on style or individuality when it comes to staying up to date with trends? Loungefly empowers you to have it all – a bag that's not only on-trend but also uniquely and authentically you. Express yourself, embrace your fandom, and carry a piece of fashion history on your arm with Loungefly. Let them take you on a trendsetting adventure that will leave you feeling stylish, confident, and undeniably cool. After all, staying ahead of the trends should always be synonymous with staying true to yourself.

Loungefly's collaborations with iconic franchises like Disney, Marvel, and Star Wars have captured the hearts of pop culture enthusiasts. These bags offer a captivating way for individuals to connect with their favourite fictional universes and proudly display their fandom. But Loungefly's appeal extends beyond the realm of fandom; they cater to a multitude of interests and hobbies. Whether you're a gaming aficionado, an art lover, or a music enthusiast, there's a Loungefly bag that perfectly aligns with your passions.

To gain deeper insights into the power of Loungefly bags as a means of self-expression, I spoke with fashion enthusiasts who shared their personal stories. Sarah, an unwavering Star Wars fan, beamed with pride as she showcased her Loungefly Star Wars backpack adorned with iconic characters and symbols from a galaxy far, far away. She described the bag as an extension of herself, saying, "When I wear this bag, it's more than just displaying my love for Star Wars. It allows me to express my individuality and showcase my unique identity. It's like carrying a piece of art that represents who I am."

Emily, an avid Disney devotee, effervescently raved about her Loungefly Mickey Mouse crossbody bag. With a sparkle in her eyes, she expressed, "Disney holds a special place in my heart, and this bag allows me to carry a little piece of that magic wherever I go. It's not just a bag; it's a conversation starter and a way for me to connect with fellow Disney enthusiasts who share the same passion."

Mark, an enthusiastic gamer, proudly dons his Loungefly backpack featuring a video game-inspired design. He shared, "Gaming is an integral part of my life, and this bag allows me to showcase my passion in a stylish and unique way. It's a conversation starter among fellow gamers, and it's a subtle nod to my interests."

What sets Loungefly bags apart is their seamless blend of fashion and self-expression. Their diverse range of designs and styles ensures that individuals can find a bag that truly reflects their personality. Whether you prefer a sleek and sophisticated design or a bold and whimsical pattern, Loungefly caters to everyone's unique tastes.

But it's not just about the bags themselves; it's about the sense of community and connection that accompanies being a Loungefly enthusiast. Sarah, Emily, and Mark all emphasised the overwhelming feeling of belonging when they spot someone else with a Loungefly bag. It's like being part of a secret club where fellow bag enthusiasts recognise and appreciate the artistry behind each design.

Loungefly bags have transcended their role as mere accessories; they have become a powerful form of self-expression. They empower individuals too proudly showcase their distinctive personality, interests, and fandoms in a stylish and fashionable way.

So, whether you're a die-hard pop culture fanatic, a fashionista searching for a statement piece, or someone who desires to carry a piece of their passion wherever they go, Loungefly bags offer the perfect avenue to express yourself and make a bold statement without uttering a single word.

So, the next time you encounter someone proudly displaying a Loungefly bag, take a moment to appreciate the artistry and self-expression behind it.

And who knows, perhaps it's time for you to join the vibrant Loungefly community and let your bag do the talking. After all, life is far too extraordinary to settle for a mundane and uninspiring bag. It's time to unleash your style and make a lasting impression with Loungefly.

Collector's Corner

When it comes to Loungefly bags, rarity reigns supreme. These are no ordinary accessories found on every store shelf. Loungefly bags are renowned for their limited editions and distinctive designs that cater to specific fandoms and pop culture franchises. Imagine possessing a bag adorned with your favourite Disney princess or Marvel superhero—such exclusivity is what we're delving into here.

Certain Loungefly designs are so rare that they become highly coveted among collectors. These sought-after bags often fetch premium prices on the vibrant secondary market, where collectors trade and sell their treasured acquisitions. Bidding wars erupt over particularly elusive designs, with collectors willing to go to great lengths to add them to their collection.
It's akin to stumbling upon a rare baseball card or a vintage comic book—the thrill of discovery amplified through the world of bags.

Here are some examples for 2023 that will go up in value(some already have)

Loungefly Princess Sketch Mini Backpack
Bag Depth: 4.5 inches
Indulge in the opulence of the Loungefly Princess Sketch Mini Backpack—a delightful fusion of style and functionality. Part of the highly sought-after Loungefly x Disney collaboration, this exquisite backpack showcases an enchanting sketch design inspired by beloved Disney Princesses.

Crafted from sumptuous vegan leather of unparalleled quality, this extraordinary backpack, valued between £80 and £130 plus depending on the retailer, effortlessly enhances any ensemble with its whimsical and distinctive charm. Its ideal dimensions make it the perfect companion for everyday use, effortlessly accommodating essentials like keys, phones, and wallets. For Disney aficionados, this backpack becomes a cherished accessory, capturing the magic and allure of their favourite characters in a truly captivating design. Featuring a well-appointed main zipper compartment, a convenient front zipper pocket, adjustable straps for personalised comfort, and a top handle for easy carrying, this backpack seamlessly combines practicality with an aura of elegance.

Photo Source: Isvouga

Monsters Inc. Boo's Door Light-up Loungefly Mini Backpack
Bag Depth: 5 inches
Discover the epitome of enchantment with the Loungefly Monsters Inc. Boo's Door Light-up Mini Backpack—an absolute must-have for devoted fans of the timeless Pixar classic! Meticulously crafted from premium vegan leather, this delightful mini backpack showcases a playful design featuring Boo's iconic door from the movie, capturing the hearts of both children and adults alike.

Unparalleled in its charm and craftsmanship, this adorable mini backpack features adjustable straps for optimal comfort, a secure top zip closure, and a surprisingly spacious interior to effortlessly accommodate all your daily essentials.

Prepare to mesmerise onlookers as the exterior boasts a captivating light-up feature, illuminating Boo's door in a mesmerising display that is sure to turn heads. This extraordinary design is a testament to Loungefly's unwavering commitment to creating unique and memorable pieces for fans of all ages.

But the magic doesn't stop there. Loungefly understands the importance of catering to all fans, regardless of their age. That's why this captivating mini backpack is also available in sizes suitable for younger movie enthusiasts, ensuring that everyone can embrace the wonder of Boo's door in their own special way.

Photo Source: https://www.popcultcha.com.au

Loungefly Disney Fantasia Character Mini Backpack - A Magical

Symphony of Style

Immerse yourself in the whimsical world of Fantasia with the Loungefly Disney Fantasia Character Mini Backpack, an officially licensed pop culture masterpiece designed by Loungefly. Crafted with meticulous attention to detail, this enchanting backpack is made from high-quality faux-leather material and features an exquisite all-over print showcasing the iconic characters from the timeless Fantasia movie.

In a regal blue hue adorned with gleaming gold hardware, this mini backpack radiates elegance and sophistication. The inclusion of a tasteful brand plaque, a front pocket, and dual side pockets adds both functionality and charm.

With dimensions of 11 3/4" x 8" x 4 1/2", this mini backpack offers the perfect canvas to transport your essentials in style. Whether you're strolling through the park, embarking on a magical adventure, or simply expressing your love for the beloved Fantasia film, this backpack allows you to carry the essence of the magical and musical journey wherever you go.

Photo Source: https://funko.com

The 50th Anniversary Luxe Logo Loungefly Backpack - A Timeless Celebration

Celebrate Loungefly's remarkable 50-year journey with the exquisite 50th Anniversary Luxe Logo Loungefly Backpack. This high-end and stylish backpack not only showcases the iconic Loungefly logo but also embodies the essence of luxury and craftsmanship. Meticulously crafted from premium materials, this backpack stands as a testament to Loungefly's unwavering commitment to quality.

The 50th Anniversary Luxe Logo Loungefly Backpack is a true collector's gem, offering intricate detailing and embroidery that elevates it to the pinnacle of Loungefly's offerings. It is a masterpiece designed to capture the hearts of fashion enthusiasts and bag connoisseurs alike.

Carry your essentials in style with this backpack, which provides ample space for keys, wallet, phone, and more. It serves as a remarkable display of your affinity for the Loungefly brand, showcasing your admiration for its heritage and dedication to impeccable design.

With a price range of £299 to £499 plus, this limited edition backpack represents a rare and highly coveted treasure for collectors. The exterior design features iconic Mickey ears and a metal "50" logo appliqué, symbolizing Loungefly's remarkable milestone. The exquisite diamond pattern, adorned with the enchanting "50" and Cinderella Castles, further adds to its allure and timeless charm.

Photo Source: https://mydisneydorks.com

Loungefly Disney Dumbo Bath Figural Mini Backpack

Step into the magical world of Disney with the charming Loungefly Disney Dumbo Bath Figural Mini Backpack. This small yet stylish backpack showcases the beloved Disney character Dumbo in an adorable "taking a bath" design. It's a delightful and whimsical accessory that will transport you back to the enchanting moments of the classic Disney film.
Designed with both fashion and functionality in mind, this mini backpack is the perfect companion for carrying your everyday essentials. Whether it's your keys, wallet, phone, or other must-have items, the Dumbo Bath Figural Mini Backpack keeps them secure and easily accessible. With its compact size and a depth of 4.5 inches, it strikes the ideal balance between convenience and style.
As you embrace your love for the timeless Disney character, this backpack becomes more than just an accessory. It's a statement piece that showcases your admiration for Dumbo and the nostalgic memories associated with the film.
The Loungefly Disney Dumbo Bath Figural Mini Backpack is available at a retail price ranging from £130 to £250, depending

on the specific design and the retailer you choose. The price reflects the exceptional quality, attention to detail, and licensing of Disney's iconic character.

Photo Source: https://spgoodssk.xyz

Loungefly Disney Princess Chibi Mini Backpack

Experience the enchantment of Disney Princesses with the delightful Loungefly Disney Princess Chibi Mini Backpack. This small, yet stylish backpack captures the essence of Disney Princesses in charming chibi versions. It's a whimsical accessory that celebrates your love for these iconic characters in a unique and fashionable way.

Designed to be both practical and trendy, this mini backpack is perfect for carrying your essential items in style. From keys and wallets to phones and more, the spacious interior with a generous 6-inch depth provides ample room for all your necessities. The adjustable straps ensure a comfortable fit, while the top zipper closure keeps your belongings secure.

Retailing from £120 to £280, the price of the Disney Princess Chibi Mini Backpack varies based on the specific design and the retailer you choose. Rest assured, the cost reflects the exceptional quality, craftsmanship, and the licensing of the beloved Disney Princess characters.

The exterior of the backpack is adorned with vibrant and colourful chibi-style artwork of the Disney Princesses. It's a captivating sight that will make any fan's heart skip a beat.

Photo Source: Pinterest

But what elevates Loungefly designs to the realm of rarity? Limited editions play a pivotal role. Loungefly frequently releases limited runs of their bags, ensuring that only a select few can possess these treasures. These limited editions often showcase special embellishments, unique materials, or collaborations with esteemed artists and beloved brands. Owning one of these gems is akin to possessing a piece of fashion history—a bag that boldly stands out from the crowd, making an unequivocal statement.

The secondary market for Loungefly bags buzzes with life, comprising a vibrant community of collectors and enthusiasts. It's a realm where buyers and sellers converge, exchanging their cherished possessions and embarking on quests to unearth those elusive designs. In this realm, bags transcend their role as mere accessories—they become symbols of dedication and passion, cherished items that hold a profound place in the collector's heart.

Highly collectible Loungefly designs:

Loungefly x Pokemon Ditto Crossbody Bag
Faux Leather Iridescent faux leather with applique and embroidered details Wipe clean; Imported Crossbody strap included Measures approximately 10 1/2-inches x 10-inches x 3-inches.
Carry your extra pokeballs in this Pokemon bag!

Photo Source: PicClick UK

And as you embark on your own collecting adventure, remain vigilant for those rare designs, limited
editions, and perhaps even hidden gems. Who knows?

You might just stumble upon the bag of your
dreams.

Happy collecting!

∞ ∞ ∞

Collecters Stories

In this section i invite you to explore the intriguing stories and insightful experiences shared by passionate collectors who have devoted their time and energy to curating extraordinary Loungefly bag collections.

I would like to acknowledgeable the below replies from the Loungefly Forum on Reddit, whose assistance was instrumental in answering these questions.

Madii

My journey into collecting began amidst the unprecedented circumstances of 2019/2020, when the COVID pandemic had a profound impact on our lives. My pastime transitioned into an immersive online shopping experience, primarily driven by a combination of circumstances and a newfound interest. Despite having noticed Loungefly products in stores like Hot Topic and BoxLunch, their appeal had eluded me, primarily due to the $70-$80 price range which seemed a significant investment at the time.

However, a particular Hocus Pocus bag piqued my interest one day, and I decided to utilise some of my BoxLunch credit to make the purchase. That decision propelled me into the expansive world of Loungefly, and I was intrigued by the sheer variety of bags available, many of which were exclusive to smaller shops. This realisation catalysed my newfound interest, and I was well on my way to becoming a dedicated collector.

Initially, the excitement led to numerous purchases, but as my collection grew, space constraints made me more selective. I began focusing more on designs that truly resonated with me, ones that I would regularly use rather than letting them gather dust. Consequently, I parted ways with pieces from my collection that did not entirely align with my preferences or were under-utilised.

My decision to start this collection was fuelled by the unique charm and innovative designs of these bags. The meticulous attention to detail, whether in the interior lining, zipper pulls, or straps, never failed to captivate me. The Hocus Pocus Blue/ Purple ombré bag was the one that started it all - the design simply caught my eye, marking my first Loungefly purchase and a significant personal investment after I transitioned to a better job.

It felt empowering to treat myself for once.

My collection might not match up to some of the incredible collections I've witnessed, but each piece is a testament to my unique taste and the fascinating journey that led me here.

StickerDragon

My journey as a collector began in 2019, ignited by an admiration for a Black Pokemon bag, which captivated me with its design. Aside from its aesthetic appeal, the bag's functional aspect was also a selling point; it was easy to carry around and manage.

Following the acquisition of my fifth bag, a thought occurred to me - why not have a unique bag for each day of the week, plus three extra for variety? With this goal in mind, I also implemented a personal rule: any desire for a new bag would be coupled with donating an unused one from my collection, or alternatively, waiting for a sale. My interest in a particular bag largely depends on its design and whether it's associated with media I'm fond of, such as Pokemon.

The black Pokemon bag, which I acquired online during a sale, marked the beginning of this collection. Even now, its charm hasn't worn off, and I find myself occasionally donning it.
My vision for the future includes the addition of more bags to my collection, which will serve as a unique wall display. Currently, I have my eyes on a Courage the Cowardly bag and an Attack on Titan bag. Among the bags I've worn, the McDonald's cross-bag has been a standout, consistently earning compliments. Its unique design and playful aesthetic have made it a personal favourite.

Her collection wasn't planned at all and already she is ten bags deep into a collection.

Picture copyright & courtesy of StickerDragon on Reddits Loungefly Forum

LoveOnceUponaTime

My initiation into the world of Loungefly began in 2020, triggered by my brother who stumbled upon a Fox and the Hound wallet he thought I'd appreciate. This led me to discover a sold-out Fox and the Hound backpack from the previous year that I found myself yearning for, along with two other bags that were almost equally enchanting. One of these was a Hot Topic preorder, the Floral Pets bag, adorned with various favourite animals of mine. The other was a white Fairies Flower backpack, depicting the playful fight between Flora and Merryweather over the colours blue and pink.

My initial purchases were these contemporary bags, after which I secured the Mini Water Fight Fox and the Hound bag I had admired, at a reasonable price on Mercari. However, my first foray into Loungefly products occurred earlier, in 2018, before Funko acquired Loungefly. It was an Eevee Tattoo print wallet, which immediately caught my fancy and soon became my preferred wallet. I cherished the experience of revealing it from my purse. Subsequently, I found a Disney Dogs Allover Print wallet on Amazon that I added to my collection.

The drive behind my collection is my deep-seated passion for art. Certain art forms incite an almost geeky enthusiasm within me. Additionally, my fondness for the online game CollecToons, a revival of Cartoon Orbit, was a contributing factor. The platform featured a vast array of images from Disney, Cartoon Network, Nickelodeon, various anime, video games, and more. It was a unique space where I truly felt at home, and its closure shortly before the pandemic left a void in my heart. This emptiness possibly fuels my desire to amass these bags, but the exquisite designs certainly play a significant role. The bags that truly resonate with me unleash my geeky side and awaken my hoarding instincts, much like Ariel from The Little Mermaid.

In my collection, the 'Eevee Heart Loungefly' bag holds a special place, as it is the only Loungefly purchase I made in person, and is associated with fond memories. Yet, the Fox and the Hound Mini Water Fight backpack is the piece that catalysed my passion for collecting.

Valerie

My Loungefly collection was conceived unintentionally during a visit to Walt Disney World (WDW) and Universal Studios in April 2023. My initial plan was to acquire a few Loungefly items as distinctive, enjoyable, and practical mementos from my vacation. To that end, I returned home with a couple of pieces. I had not intended to amass a collection; these were simply meant to be keepsakes from my trip.

However, upon purchasing my first Loungefly item, I found myself taken aback by their quality and delightful nature. Further, transitioning from a purse to a backpack was a change I found surprisingly agreeable. The items' dual functionality – both practical for daily use and aesthetically pleasing as decorative pieces – only added to their appeal. As I began to display them around my bedroom, I realised the joy I derived from looking at them was equal to that of carrying them around.

The decision to purchase the silver Disney 100 bag occurred at WDW's High School. It immediately struck me as a perfect souvenir that would always serve as a vivid reminder of our trip. Its shimmering aesthetic was equally captivating. Our visit to Universal and the Islands of Adventure the following day saw the addition of Jurassic Park and Harry Potter Loungefly items to my collection.

An intriguing incident occurred at one of Universal's stores when my son selected a Jurassic World toy that was seemingly priced exorbitantly. A quick online search revealed that the toy was available on Amazon at half the price. This prompted me to check the Loungefly website to ensure that I wasn't overpaying for my bag. To my delight, I discovered a significant sale which led me to order four more bags and wallets on the spot, even as I was in line to purchase my Jurassic Park bag.

Though my acquisitions spanned over two days and involved more than one bag, I consider all of this as my first purchase, particularly because it was initially meant to mark both the beginning and end of my Loungefly acquisitions. Little did I know then, that this was the genesis of a growing collection.

Photo Copyright and courtesy of Valerie from the Reddit Loungefly Forum

Photo Credit: RaShelle Pulsipher

Picture credit: Dolci Di Amie Cake Studio

Below is some of my Wife's collection

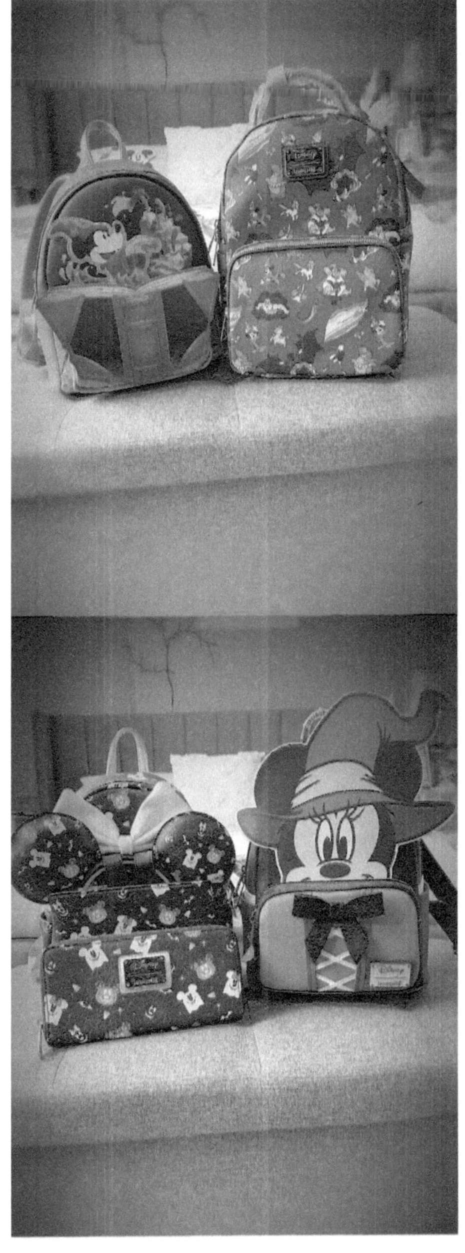

Pic credit : Kennedy Lane

Picture Credit: Toria

Photo Credit: Judy Campos

Loungefly Bag Care Guide: Ensuring Longevity and Beauty

For the dedicated Loungefly aficionados among us, maintaining the pristine condition and longevity of these sought-after accessories is paramount. Recognising the unparalleled quality of Loungefly bags and their potential to endure, this guide provides specialized care instructions. By understanding the makeup of these bags and following a few essential care steps, your treasured items can remain timeless.

Material Insight:
Loungefly bags predominantly use Faux Vegan Leather, a robust material crafted from polyurethane. This substance boasts durability and can be maintained with relative ease.

Initial Care:
Before diving into a detailed cleaning regimen, initiate the process by wiping the bag with a dry microfibre cloth. Regardless of whether it's been stored in its original packaging, the bag could have residues from manufacturing or have been exposed to dust, oils, or even cosmetics. This initial wipe ensures you're working with a clean surface.

Cleaning Methods:
While Faux Vegan Leather is generally low-maintenance, periodic cleaning can help in preserving its lustre. Here are two methods:

METHOD #1: Gentle Cleaning
1. Empty the accessory.
2. Combine warm water and a pea-sized amount of liquid soap or mild detergent in a bowl or bucket. Immerse a soft towel in this solution, ensuring excess water is squeezed out. Gently wipe away stains using this damp towel.
3. Dry the accessory with a microfibre cloth and allow it to air dry fully.

Note: While effective, refrain from frequent use of this method, as it could gradually diminish the bag's shine.

METHOD #2: Specialised Cleaning
1. Start by removing any residues, oils, or particles using a

microfibre cloth.

2. Using leather cleaning kits (we recommend the Coach Product Care Kit), apply a small portion to a clean cloth and work it onto the bag in circular motions.

3. Clear of residues with a microfibre cloth and let it air dry for approximately 30 minutes.

4. Enhance the leather's shine by applying a dollop of Coach Leather Moisturiser to a cloth, rubbing it onto the leather in circular patterns.

5. Remove excess with a microfibre cloth and let it sit and air dry for another 30 minutes.

Pro Tips:

- For weekly maintenance, consider using alcohol-free baby wipes. However, be wary; not all faux leathers react the same to different products.
- Prior to using any cleaning product, perform a patch test in a discreet area of the accessory. Wait a few minutes to confirm there's no colour alteration.
- Machine washing is a strict no-go for Loungefly accessories; it reduces their lifespan considerably.

- Organisers are excellent investments for those who carry cosmetics, writing tools, or other potential stain-causing items in their bags.
Not only do they protect the interior lining, but they also ensure your bags remain organised. Numerous options are available on

platforms like Amazon and eBay, catering to various preferences and sizes.

You can explore a range of backpack organiser inserts tailored for your Loungefly bag on platforms like Amazon and eBay. These inserts help in neatly arranging the contents of your bag for ease of access.

For those looking to protect their bags and accessories from dust and potential damage, Linyapry offers transparent storage boxes. These are conveniently available for purchase on both Amazon and eBay.

If you wish to elegantly showcase your favourite Funko Loungefly Mini Backpack, idisplayit.co.uk provides robust acrylic display boxes. These display cases ensure your backpack remains pristine, safeguarded from dust and external elements.

There is also a Songmics 16 cube storage unit you can purchase on Amazon for less than £16.

You can choose between sleek white or classic black designs. Priced at approximately £40 each, these displays typically have a delivery timeframe of 2 weeks from the seller.

By following this guide, you ensure your Loungefly treasures stay in impeccable condition, ready to complement your style for years to come.

General places where fans of specific brands or products, including Loungefly, gather:

1. **Reddit:** There are dedicated subreddits for Loungefly fans. For example, r/Loungefly or broader communities related to accessories or pop culture where Loungefly is discussed.

2. **Facebook Groups:** Facebook often has groups dedicated to specific brands or interests. Simply search "Loungefly" in the search bar, and you'll likely find buy/sell/trade groups, fan appreciation groups, and more.

3. **Instagram:** Use hashtags like #Loungefly, #LoungeflyForSale, or #LoungeflyCollector to discover posts and communities focused on Loungefly. There might be dedicated pages or sellers promoting their products here.

4. **Discord Servers:** Discord isn't just for gamers. Many fan communities create servers for specific interests, and there might be one for Loungefly fans.

5. **Forums and Websites:** Some fan bases might have dedicated websites or forums. While these are becoming less common in the age of social media, it's still possible for niche interests.

6. **eBay and Mercari:** While these are primarily platforms for buying and selling, they can sometimes serve as de facto forums. Users often share information, ask questions in the product

listings, or even form communities around specific interests.

7. **PurseForum:** This is a broad forum dedicated to purses, but there are discussions about various brands, including Loungefly.

To find the most current and active communities, a simple Google search along the lines of "Loungefly fan forums" or "Loungefly buy & sell groups" might yield the best results. Remember always to be cautious when joining online groups or making transactions, ensuring your privacy and safety.

Where to Find Loungefly Backpacks at Disney World U.S.A

- World of Disney (Disney Springs)
- The Emporium (Main Street, U.S.A)
- Beverly Sunset Boutique (Sunset Blvd)
- Disney Clothiers (Main Street, U.S.A)
- Memento Mori's (Liberty Square)
- Star Traders (Tomorrowland)
- Disney Style (Disney Springs)
- Gateway Gifts (Epcot)
- ImageWorks (Epcot)
- Black Spire Outpost (Galaxy's Edge)
- Star Wars Trading Post (Disney Springs)
- Disney's Art of Animation Resort
- Disney's Riviera Resort
- SuperHero Headquarters (Disney Springs)

Authorised list of Loungefly small shops, U.S.A

707 Street
8Twenty3 Boutique
8Twenty3boutique.com
A Comic Spot
AJ's Express Boutique
Adorn Purse & Co.
Alchemy Hair Design
All That & More
Ambrie
Attic Salt
Baby Geekery
Baby Rabiez
Barker Animation Art Gallery
BarkerAnimation.com
Bedrock City Comic Company
Bedrockcity Comics
Bibbidi
Big Bad Toy Store
Blashful
Blue Culture Tees
Boodee, Inc
Boten LLC dba Fundmoriginal
Brads Toys and Collectibles
Broadway Pinups
Cosmic Corner
Captain's Comics
Casay LLC
Central Florida Novelty and Gifts
Character World
Chico Princess Parties
Christy's Toy Chest
Chrono Toys

Mor's & Co. at Fontainebleau Miami Beach
Mouse Marketplace
My Awesome Collectibles
Mythical Mountain
Needzo Inc
NefariousCollectibles.com
Nerdalee.com
Nichole Madison Boutique
No Limit Gaming
OC Collectibles
Oh Fun Shop
Ooh La La Candles
Open and Clothing
Owley Boutique
Park Bench Threads
Party & Gift Outlet Inc.
Peppermint Park Miami
Pin-Up Bootique
Pink a la Mode
Pins Break The Internet
Pixie Pop Up
Planetary Toys
Plastic Empire
Play On Collectibles
Poly's Comics
Pop's Comics & Collectibles
Pops n Sons
Pretty Things VIP
Pro Toys LLC
PurejoyToys.net
Quips N Quotes
Rainbow Cloudz

Circle Of Hope
CnP Alley
Coco's Monkey
Collectables N Stuff Collectibles
Collection Lounge
Collectors Outlet
Comic Cove
Comicbookclothing.com
Cordy's Corner
DOC's Unique Collectibles
Dan;s Sports Cards & Games
Dark Delicacies
Deckers Fine Gifts
Dekko Store
Department of the Interior
Diplo USA Inc.
Disney Pins Blog
Doc's Unique Collectibles
Dragonfly Shops and Gardens
E 68th Street
Eight3Five
Emerald City Collectibles
Enchanted Toy
EnchantedSuppliers.com
Endless Summer Tattoo
Espi Lane
Express Gadget
FTW Game Co.
Factory Xtreme
Fancy
Fantastic Collectibles
Fearless Apparel
Feather & Vine
Ferarra Box
First Capitol Trading

Razorz Edge
Red Five Toys & Collectibles
Replay Toys LLC
Retro Reset Video Games &
Sunshine Daydream
SW Seller
Sanica Enterprise
Sanrio Arcadia
Sanrio Irvine
Sanrio Monrovia
Sanrio Surprises
Sanrio Tyler
Sapphire Sky Boutique
Savvy's Boutique
Sharing Magical Moments
Shoe Central
Shop Merch Ventures
Shop Sara Jane
Shop Shiny Shopper
Shop Zimo
ShopPopOnline
Sourpuss Clothing
Southcoastbabyco.com
Spell Boutique
Star's Toys
Studio 10 Fifteen
Sugar & Spiked Beautique
Super Hero Stuff
Superherostuff.com
Sure Things Toys
Surf and Dirt
Sweet Stylinn Boutique
TD Collectibles LLC
THE LUNYX SHOOP
TK Ave

Forever PB & J
Forget Me Not Boutique
Freaky Findz
Fugitive Toys
Fun.Com
Gacha Mart
Gallery of Art & Collectibles Inc.
GoPin Pro
Green Lotus Dreams
Greg Yantz Pins
Grotto Tresaures
Halloween town
Hammergirl Anime
Happy 8 Collectibles
Happy Mile Style
Hollywood Heroes and Villains
Homewood Toy & Hobby Shop
House of Cars and Toys
Howard Johnston Anaheim
IDS Entertainment
Ichi Trading Corp
Icon Sports and Novelty
Jr's Sports
Julie's Gifts and Accesories
Kappa Toys
Kawaii Gists
Keith's Comics
Kola-pop.com
Kraken Trade
Kryptonite Character Store
Kryptonite Kollectibles
La Style Rush
Landrosells
Larger Than Life Toys and Comics
Lewis Galleries
Lonestar Finds

TK Innovation
The Burrow
The Hob Nob Shop
The Line Jumper
The Mad Bagger
The Queen's Quarry
The Rabbit Hole Trading Co.
The Shoe Attic
Three Little Mingos
ToyCyndicate, LLC
ToyznFun
TrinketEars (Premier SouvenEars)
Twin Treats Boutique
Under The Sea Collectibles
Unlock The Con
UrbanPro
Value Crown
Very Neko
Vrare
Walkerroseboutique.com
Wednesddayshoppe
Whimsical Wishes
Witness The Fear
World 1-1 Games
World Class Deals, LLC
Your WDW Store
Zobie Productions

Luggage Factory
Lulabites
Luxebag
Mad Mod Shop
Mars & Venus Emporium Canada
Martin and Macarthur
Merch Ventures
Mickey Monthly
Modern Pinup

UK & Ireland Authorised Loungefly Stockists

- Amazon
- Angela Bare
- Be More Geek
- Branded Toys
- Burton Blake
- Cool! Merchandise
- Damaged Society
- EMP
- Forbidden Planet International
- Forbidden Planet Limited
- Freak Treat
- Freemans
- FunkoEurope.com
- Funky Figures
- Gadget Station
- Geek Garage
- Geek merchandise
- Geekcore
- Get Ready Comics
- Glamglass Gifts
- Hamleys
- Harrods
- Hive
- HMV
- Hooks UK
- House Of Fraser
- Hull Pops
- Just Geek
- Koolaz
- LF Lovers
- Live & Exclusive
- Lord Collectables
- Mad-4-Toys
- Magic Madhouse
- Menkind
- Merchoid
- Nerd Base
- Pop Figures
- Prezzybox
- Razmatazz
- Retro Nation
- Retro Styler
- Rockamilly
- Television And Movie Store
- The Disney Store
- The Film Cell
- The Movie Shack
- Toy Hut
- TruffleShuffle
- Yachew
- Yella Brick Road
- Zalando
- Zatu Games
- Zinga Entertainment

Authorised Stockists In Czech Republic, Poland, Switzerland & North Macedonia

EMP
Funkoeurope.com
Xzone
Zalando

EMP
Empik
Funkoeurope.com
Zalando

_

EMP
Funkoeurope.com
Genki
Itsumademo
Zalando

—

EMP
Funkoeurop.com
Literatura.mk
Zalando

Authorised Stockists In France

Addict Popculture
Cadeaucity
Chez Clochette Boutique
EMP
Find'N'Geek
FNAC
Funkeurope.com
Geekcore
Geekotheque
Generation Disney
Get Ready Comics
Good'IN'
La Cite Magique
LF Lovers
Micromania
Pop Figures
Pulp's
Shopforgeek
TruffleShuffle
Zalando

Authorised Stockists In Germany

EMP
Elbenwald
Funkoeurope.com
Gamestop
Geekcore
Get Ready Comics
Hunter & Collectors
Kadewe
LF Lovers
Nerdy Terdy Gang
Pop Figures
Qingstore
TruffleShuffle
X-Comics
Zalando

Authorised Stockists In Benelux

4Geeks
De Popshop
Derwin Collectables

EMP
Funkoeurope.com
Kings & Queens
Le Reliquaire
LF Lovers
Magical Gifts
Mickey's Gifts
Moon Collectibles
Neverland Shop
Pop Figures
Shop For Geek
Smartoys
Succubus
The Neverland
TruffleShuffle
Zalando

Authorised stockists in Spain & Portugal

Comic Stores
EMP
Endorshop
Freakland
Funkoeurope.com

Geekcore
Get Ready Comics
LF Lovers
Loja Dos Pop's
Pop Figures
Raccon Games
The Time Seller
TruffleShuffle
Zalando

Authorised Stockists in Italy, Greece & Denmark

EMP
Funkeurope.com
Geekcore
Get Ready Comics
LF Lovers
Pop Figures
TruffleShuffle
Zalando

Games Academy
Gamestop
Mini Big World Collectibles

Nerdom
Nowloading

Faraos

Epilogue

Summary condensed version of Loungefly for a quick read.

Guide to Loungefly Mini Backpacks

When exploring the magical world of Disney parks, a plethora of enchanting souvenirs will undoubtedly pique your interest. Among them, the Loungefly mini backpacks stand out as the ultimate Disney keepsake. But what sets these bags apart?

Understanding Loungefly Bags

Loungefly, a subsidiary of Funko, crafts products inspired by pop culture, ranging from pins and lanyards to wallets and Minnie ears. As of 2023, they've even teamed up with Hipdot to introduce makeup palettes. Among their myriad offerings, their mini backpacks are particularly prized, representing the most sought-after souvenir in the Disney parks.

These mini backpacks capture the essence of numerous franchises including Disney (encompassing Marvel and Star Wars), Pokémon, Ghostbusters, Studio Ghibli, Harry Potter, and many more.

Why Are Loungefly Products Collectible?

Loungefly items are distinctive due to their limited availability. Once a design has been in circulation for a certain duration, it's phased out, ensuring a fresh array of designs in the market. Some are exclusives, crafted specifically for certain retailers. For instance, certain Disney park Loungefly bags are exclusive to the parks and ShopDisney.com.

Decoding Loungefly Jargon

For those new to Loungefly collecting, here are some key terms to familiarise yourself with:

- **AOP (All Over Print)**: Refers to designs printed haphazardly all over a bag.
- **Placement**: Refers to the positioning of the design, especially on the front pocket.
- **Chibi**: A character design resembling a Funko pop, characterised by exaggerated heads and tiny bodies.
- **Cosplay Bags**: Designs mimicking a character's face or attire.
- **Grail**: A highly desired bag, either personally or within the community.
- **HTF**: An abbreviation for 'Hard To Find'.
- **MMMA/MTMA**: Initialisms relating to themed merchandise releases from Disney parks.

Evaluating Quality and Retailers

Quality often correlates with the type of plaque on a Loungefly bag. Higher-end bags sport metal plaques, indicative of padded straps and unique linings. These are primarily available at Disney parks, BoxLunch, and select retailers. On the other hand, bags with fabric plaques—typically found at Hot Topic and occasionally at smaller retailers—lack these enhanced features.

Exclusivity also plays a role in determining value. Many retailers, including Disney parks, BoxLunch, and Loungefly.com, have their own exclusive designs. To stay updated on exclusives, subscribing to retailers' email lists and following their Instagram accounts is advisable.

Determining Rarity and Value

To assess a bag's rarity or market value, consider:

- **Plaque Design**: Bags produced before Funko's 2018 acquisition of Loungefly have a heart logo, marking them as more

rare and desired.
- **Market Research**: Explore platforms like Mercari to ascertain current market prices, focusing on sold listings.
- **Unique Manufacturing Flaws**: Some bags might feature plaques positioned upside down, rendering them rarer and potentially more valuable.

Are Loungefly Bags Plus-Size Friendly?

Absolutely! For those seeking maximum comfort:

- Opt for bags post-Funko acquisition, identifiable by the non-heart logo plaques.
- Prioritise bags with padded straps, typically absent on fabric plaque designs.
- Bags with strap bases on the sides, rather than the bottom, are preferable.
- Sequinned bags might cause discomfort due to scratchiness.
- Loungefly's new exchangeable straps offer plus-size options, although currently limited to purses.

In essence, for optimal comfort, it's wise to avoid bags with the heart logo or fabric plaques, but again that is down to personal preference.

Afterword

Acknowledgment of Errors

In the pursuit of knowledge and the chronicling of stories, even with the best intentions and efforts, oversights may occur. It is with a profound sense of responsibility that I acknowledge any inaccuracies, errors, or omissions that may be present in this book. They are, in entirety, my own.

While every effort has been made to ensure the accuracy and completeness of the information contained within these pages, the dynamic nature of knowledge and human fallibility means imperfections are inevitable. I am deeply appreciative of the readers and experts in the field who engage with this work, and I welcome constructive feedback and corrections.

Your understanding and patience, as you embark on this journey with me, is both valued and cherished. I am committed to continuous learning, and any subsequent editions of this book will aim to rectify acknowledged errors. Thank you for your support and trust.

Contact me if you would like to be included in my next book: contactme@aiqbalauthor.com

About The Author

Asaf Iqbal

A resident of Shropshire, has embarked on an exciting new journey in 2023 as he introduces his books to the world.

With a passion for writing that spans years, Asaf is thrilled to share his literary creations. Alongside his roles as a father and a grandfather, he indulges in the pleasures of watching movies and TV shows, as well as collecting props and autographs from his favourite films and series.

Staying active and exploring new destinations also holds a special place in his heart, providing inspiration for his writing endeavours. You can visit his website at https://www.aiqbalauthor.com (Coming Soon), where he will feature a blog to keep his loyal readers updated on his book series, new releases, cherished reads, and engage in meaningful connections.

Discovering Disneyland Paris: Tips And Tricks For Beginners

Discovering Disneyland Paris: Tips and Tricks for Beginners is your ultimate guide to unlocking the magic of the most enchanting theme park in Europe. Whether you're a first-time visitor or seeking to enhance your Disneyland Paris experience, this comprehensive book is packed with insider knowledge, expert advice, and essential tips to make the most of your trip.

Embark on a journey through the enchanting lands of Disneyland Paris as you uncover hidden gems, navigate queues like a pro, and discover the secrets to maximising your time and enjoyment. From Main Street's nostalgic charm to the thrilling adventures of Frontierland, from the fairy tale wonders of Fantasyland to the exotic escapades of Adventureland, this guide will lead you through every corner of the park.

Inside, you'll find practical strategies for planning your visit, including advice on ticket options, accommodations & dining. Unveil the best times to visit, discover strategies for avoiding crowds, and learn how to make the most of your favourite attractions. Uncover hidden features & insights that will truly immerse you in the Disneyland Paris experience.

Featuring insider tips from experienced Disney travellers, this book is your passport to a magical adventure. Whether you're seeking thrilling rides, unforgettable entertainment, or immersive storytelling, Discovering Disneyland Paris: Tips and Tricks for Beginners is the essential companion for creating memories that will last a lifetime.

Prepare to embark on a journey like no other as you unravel the wonders of Disneyland Paris, armed with the knowledge and expertise that will make your visit truly extraordinary. Get ready to unlock the secrets, conquer the queues, and create your own unforgettable story at the happiest place on Earth.

The Correct Mindset To Start A Home Based Business

This book reveals the key principles for cultivating the right mindset to overcome obstacles, develop resilience, and tap into your full potential. Unleash the entrepreneur within and embark on a journey of growth, productivity, and fulfillment as you build your thriving home-based business.

Whether you're a budding entrepreneur seeking the confidence to take the leap or an established business owner looking to recalibrate your mindset, this book serves as a trusted guide to foster the right mental framework for home-based business success.

Are you ready to unlock the keys to success from within? Let this book be your companion as you embark on a transformative quest to build a thriving home-based business.

Rise And Lift: A Contemporary Approach To Weight Training

Unleash Your Strength. Ignite Your Potential.

In Rise and Lift: A Contemporary Approach to Weight Training, discover a dynamic and transformative guide that takes you on a modern journey into the world of weightlifting. From beginners seeking a fresh start to fitness enthusiasts craving a new perspective, this book empowers you to embark on a lifting journey that will reshape your body, mind, and life.

Step-by-step, you'll master the fundamental principles of weightlifting, uncovering the secrets of proper form, technique, and safety. Dive into the depths of progressive overload and learn how to unlock your body's hidden strength. With an array of lifting techniques, innovative training programs, and comprehensive guidance on nutrition and recovery, you'll find yourself equipped with all the tools needed to sculpt a powerful physique.

But it's not just about physical gains. 'Rise and Lift' recognizes the intrinsic connection between mental and physical well-being. Uncover the mindset and motivation required to overcome obstacles, stay consistent, and achieve lasting results. Immerse yourself in inspiring real-life stories of transformation, and let them fuel your determination to rise above limitations.

Whether you seek to build strength, sculpt muscles, or enhance your overall fitness, Rise and Lift presents a contemporary approach that caters to all ages and genders. Prepare to witness your body and spirit soar to new heights as you embrace weightlifting as a transformative path to unleash your true potential.

Get ready to rise above. Get ready to lift.

5 Businesses To Start From Home : From Home To Success: Empowering Entrepreneurs With 5 Lucrative Business Ideas

Are you tired of the daily grind and yearning for a more flexible and fulfilling work life?

Look no further!

5 Businesses To Start From Home is your guide to unleashing your entrepreneurial spirit from the comfort of your own home.

This comprehensive book takes you on a journey of exploration, presenting five proven and lucrative business ideas that can be successfully operated without ever leaving your doorstep.

From online ventures to service-based enterprises, each chapter delves into the practical steps, strategies, and tools you need to start and grow your own thriving home-based business.

Discover the freedom, autonomy, and financial potential that awaits you as you embark on this exciting path. Whether you're a stay-at-home parent, a budding entrepreneur, or simply seeking additional income streams, this book empowers you to turn your dreams into reality.

Take charge of your future and unlock the boundless possibilities of home-based entrepreneurship today!

Love And Longing

Mia needs to get her life together. She had everything right on paper.

A great job, a beautiful house, excellent friends, and a 'loving' fiancé. But life isn't what it seems on the outside.

What started as a perfect romance soon became a nightmare. Now she's stuck in a rut, with a man who isn't right for her at all. And she's looking for a way out.

But will she find one?

Perhaps a handsome stranger with eyes as blue as the sky is exactly what she needs to help her realise that.

Love and longing brings you a heartwarming tale of how 'love' can imprison you, but true love can set you free.

A Guide To Mastering Household Bills & Finances: 2023 Edition

This book was written to help individuals and families reclaim control over their finances and navigate the often overwhelming world of budgeting and saving.

From reducing household bills to maximising government assistance programs, this book equips readers with the tools they need to make informed financial decisions and create lasting positive change in their lives.

If you're ready to take charge of your financial well-being and unlock a world of possibilities.

Get ready to transform your financial outlook, one decision at a time.

Autograph Collecting: A Beginners Guide

In "A Beginner's Guide to Autograph Collecting," you can embark on a journey to explore this fascinating world and learn the ropes of building your own autograph collection. Whether you're a seasoned collector or just starting out, this book is packed with valuable insights, practical tips, and expert advice to help you navigate the intricacies of autograph collecting.

Discover the significance of autographs as unique personal possessions and their broader cultural and historical importance. Learn about the different methods of obtaining autographs, including in-person encounters, through the mail, auctions, and estate sales. Explore the thrill of hunting down rare autographs and discover the potential for investment in this captivating hobby.

Authenticity is key when it comes to autograph collecting, and this book will provide you with valuable insights into the authentication process. Uncover advanced techniques and strategies for long-term collection building, ensuring the preservation and value of your prized autographs.

Whether you're captivated by the historical significance, the thrill of the hunt, or the personal connection to your favorite personalities, this guide is your passport to creating a collection that will be cherished for generations to come.

Start your autograph collecting journey today and unlock a world of extraordinary possibilities.